W9-BYL-720

SAVING THE GRIZZLY BEAR

by Karen Latchana Kenney

po**g**o

Ideas for Parents and Teachers

Pogo Books let children practice reading informational text while introducing them to nonfiction features such as headings, labels, sidebars, maps, and diagrams, as well as a table of contents, glossary, and index.

Carefully leveled text with a strong photo match offers early fluent readers the support they need to succeed.

Before Reading

- "Walk" through the book and point out the various nonfiction features. Ask the student what purpose each feature serves.
- Look at the glossary together. Read and discuss the words.

Read the Book

- Have the child read the book independently.
- Invite him or her to list questions that arise from reading.

After Reading

- Discuss the child's questions. Talk about how he or she might find answers to those questions.
- Prompt the child to think more. Ask: Grizzly bears are an important North American animal. Why do you think we need them?

Pogo Books are published by Jump!
5357 Penn Avenue South
Minneapolis, MN 55419
www.jumplibrary.com

Library of Congress Cataloging-in-Publication Data

Names: Kenney, Karen Latchana, author.
Title: Saving the grizzly bear / by Karen Latchana Kenney.
Description: Minneapolis, MN : Jump!, Inc., [2019]
Series: Great animal comebacks | Audience: Ages 7-10.
Includes bibliographical references and index.
Identifiers: LCCN 2018034354 (print)
LCCN 2018035656 (ebook)
ISBN 9781641282871 (ebook)
ISBN 9781641282864 (hardcover : alk. paper)
Subjects: LCSH: Grizzly bear–Juvenile literature.
Rare mammals–Juvenile literature.
Wildlife conservation–Juvenile literature.
Classification: LCC QL737.C27 (ebook)
LCC QL737.C27 K478 2019 (print) | DDC 599.784–dc23
LC record available at https://lccn.loc.gov/2018034354

Editor: Jenna Trnka
Designer: Anna Peterson

Photo Credits: ricochet64/iStock, cover; Manamana/Shutterstock, 1, 12-13; robert cicchetti/Shutterstock, 3; ArCaLu/Shutterstock, 4; Twildlife/Dreamstime, 5; Scott E Read/Shutterstock, 6-7; Paul Souders/Getty, 8-9; Kelly vanDellen/Shutterstock, 10; Craighead Institute, 11; MPH Photos/Shutterstock, 14-15; Amelia Martin/Dreamstime, 15; Pep Roig/Alamy, 16-17; zixian/Shutterstock, 18; Andrew Morehouse/Dreamstime, 19; Chase Dekker/Dreamstime, 20-21; Gammal/Shutterstock, 23.

Printed in the United States of America at Corporate Graphics in North Mankato, Minnesota.

TABLE OF CONTENTS

CHAPTER 1

FEARED GRIZZLIES

It is springtime in the Rocky Mountains. A mother grizzly bear walks with her **cubs**. She teaches them to find food.

cubs ····▶

Grizzly bears are **omnivores**. They are a **keystone species**. They help keep nature in balance. But they became **threatened**.

European settlers moved west in the 1800s. They cleared bear **habitats** for farmland. They set up bear traps. They shot and killed grizzlies, too. Why?

People feared the bears. They did not want to be attacked. And they did not want the bears to kill their **livestock**.

DID YOU KNOW?

Grizzly bears are fierce. And very large! They can weigh around 800 pounds (360 kilograms) each! That's about as heavy as three large refrigerators!

By the mid-1900s, only small **populations** were left. And only in certain areas. Some lived in Glacier and Yellowstone **National Parks**. They stayed safe in the mountains. There, they were far from people.

TAKE A LOOK!

Grizzly bears once lived from northern Alaska into Mexico. Close to 100,000 of them! Now they live in northern parts of North America. Most live in western Canada and Alaska.

NORTH AMERICA

■ = historic grizzly bear range

■ = current grizzly bear range

CHAPTER 2

SAVING THE GRIZZLY

Grizzlies were protected in Yellowstone. No one could hunt animals there. Two brothers began studying grizzlies in the park. When? In 1958. It was the first time scientists studied them.

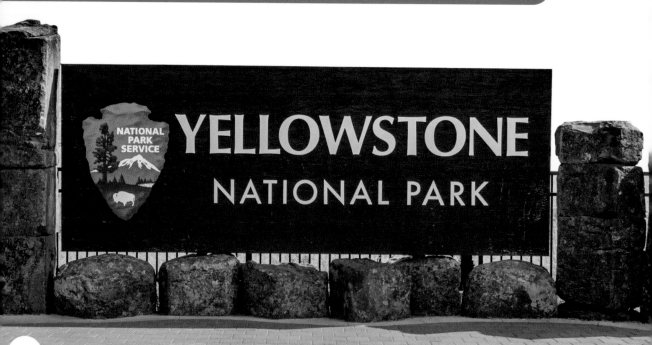

NATIONAL PARK SERVICE

YELLOWSTONE
NATIONAL PARK

radio collar ·····▶

Frank and John Craighead used **radio collars** to track the bears. People wrote about the scientists. And made movies. Millions of people learned about their work. They saw how these **apex predators** helped keep nature in balance.

By the mid-1970s, only 800 to 1,000 **grizzly bears** were left in the lower 48 states. The government stepped in to help.

They put the bears on the **endangered species** list. When? In 1975. This made it illegal to hunt the bears. Where? Everywhere. Not just national parks.

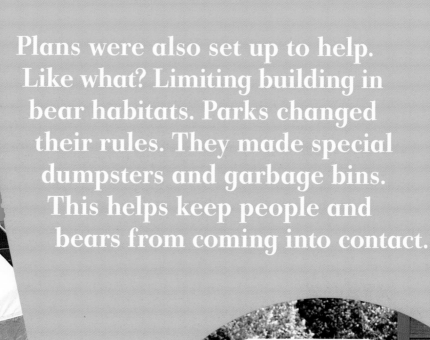

Plans were also set up to help. Like what? Limiting building in bear habitats. Parks changed their rules. They made special dumpsters and garbage bins. This helps keep people and bears from coming into contact.

bear-proof garbage bin

They also made poles. Why? So campers can hang up their food. This makes it harder for the bears to get. So fewer bears come near people.

Slowly, grizzly bear numbers rose. Between 1,200 to 1,400 grizzly bears live in the lower 48 states now.

DID YOU KNOW?

Grizzly bears are always looking for food. Even in garbage bins and dumpsters. If food is left out, the bears come close to people.

CHAPTER 3

GRIZZLY BEARS IN THE WILD

Many grizzlies live in the Rocky Mountains. And along the Pacific Coast. Each fall, they eat as much as they can to prepare for **hibernation**. They catch salmon. They also eat deer, elk, moose, and bison.

salmon

Grizzly populations have grown. The ones in the Yellowstone area were taken off the endangered species list. Now people can hunt them in some states.

As they roam, they may meet people. People are the bears' biggest threats. But grizzly bears don't need to be killed. Electric fences keep them away from livestock and garbage. Bear-proof garbage bins help, too. With our help, these bears can remain in the wild. They can continue to be a keystone species.

DID YOU KNOW?

If you see a grizzly, do not run. Walk away slowly. Stay calm. And be prepared. Bear spray can keep them away if they get close. It is always best to give them their space.

ACTIVITIES & TOOLS

TRY THIS!

LISTENING TO GRIZZLIES

If you hear a grizzly bear, it is because the bear is nervous or angry. Listen to some of the sounds a grizzly bear makes.

What You Need:
- computer
- notebook
- pen

① Ask an adult to help you visit this website on a computer:
- **Sound Library, Grizzly Bear:** https://www.nps.gov/yell/learn/photosmultimedia/grizzlysounds.htm

② Listen to the different sounds on the site. Take notes as you listen. What do the sounds remind you of? Do you notice patterns to their sounds?

③ Compare the different roars, huffs, and popping sounds. How are they different? How are they the same? Can you make some grizzly bear sounds?

GLOSSARY

apex predators: Predators at the top of a food chain that are not hunted by any other animal.

cubs: Young bears.

endangered species: A plant or animal that is in danger of becoming extinct.

habitats: The places and natural conditions in which animals or plants live.

hibernation: The act of spending the winter sleeping or resting.

keystone species: A species of plant or animal that has a major impact on and is essential to the ecosystem in which it belongs.

livestock: Animals that are kept or raised on a farm or ranch.

national parks: Large sections of land that are protected by the federal government for people to visit and to preserve wildlife.

omnivores: Animals that eat both plants and meat.

populations: The total numbers of living things in certain areas.

radio collars: Collars placed on animals that send radio signals out to scientists, who use them to track the animals.

threatened: Likely to become an endangered species.

INDEX

TO LEARN MORE

Finding more information is as easy as 1, 2, 3.

1. Go to www.factsurfer.com
2. Enter "savingthegrizzlybear" into the search box.
3. Click the "Surf" button to see a list of websites.

FACT SURFER